WORDS IN ACTION
FINDING THE RIGHT WORDS

WORDS IN ACTION
FINDING THE RIGHT WORDS

The Institute Series | 11

THE HEYTHROP INSTITUTE FOR RELIGION, ETHICS & PUBLIC LIFE

HEYTHROP INSTITUTE FOR RELIGION, ETHICS & PUBLIC LIFE

Published by the Heythrop Institute
for Religion, Ethics & Public Life

Heythrop College
Kensington Square
London W8 5HQ

http//www.heythrop.ac.uk/HIREPL

© Heythrop Institute for Religion, Ethics &
Public Life 2008

This book is in copyright. Subject to statutory
exception and to the provisions of relevant collective
licensing agreements, no reproduction of any part
may take place without the written permission of the
Heythrop Institute for Religion, Ethics & Public Life.

First published 2008

Printed in Belgium at Lithos Printing,
Wommelgem, Antwerp

Designed by Frederik Hulstaert, Antwerp

A catalogue reference for this book is
available from the British Library

ISBN 978-1-905566-10-5

CONTENTS

7   Introduction
    Patrick Riordan SJ
    Associate Director, The Heythrop Institute for Religion, Ethics & Public Life

13 Voluntary, Religious and Faith-Based Organizations:
    Some Important Distinctions
    Malcolm Torry
    *Team Rector in the East Greenwich Team Ministry
    and Site Chaplain with the Greenwich Peninsula Chaplaincy*

31 At a Loss for Words
    Patrick Riordan SJ
    Associate Director, The Heythrop Institute for Religion, Ethics & Public Life

47 Echoes of the Other –
    The Cultural and Religious Roots of Philanthropy
    Michael Barnes SJ
    Teaches Inter-religious Relations at Heythrop College

INTRODUCTION

THIS ISSUE OF THE INSTITUTE SERIES subtitled 'Finding the right words' is a further contribution to the Words in Action project. Number 10 in the series was subtitled 'Speaking in our own words' and the papers collected there illustrated some of the resources available from faith traditions for speaking of charitable activity in the public domain. They illustrated also the distinctiveness of the language which is rooted in a faith perspective. There is a slight shift in focus in the three papers collected in this volume. There is more of an acknowledgment that there can be a difficulty in finding the right words to express who we are and what we do in faith-based charitable organizations. There can be many sources of that difficulty, not least the complexity of the situations with which we have to deal, as well as our own lack of competence and mastery of the appropriate language. There is in addition the confusion which arises because we must operate in different languages.

Dr Malcolm Torry offers some guidance through the complexity by presenting and elaborating a series of important distinctions which are relevant for those who find themselves placed in conversations across relevant boundaries. The mere listing of the distinctions which he explores is sufficient to highlight the difficulty of achieving clarity and of finding the right words. Making a list of the distinctions conveys the message in a visual manner.

> Distinctions
> Voluntary and religious organizations
> Religious and faith-based organizations
> 'Attached' and 'wandering' faith-based organizations
> The secular and the religious
> The public sector and the voluntary sector
> The public sector and the religious sector.

Religious- and faith-based organizations must be concerned with the criterion of 'public benefit' if they are to qualify as charities in the sense of the Charity Act 2006, just as they are challenged to deal with the public policy goals of 'inclusion' and 'social cohesion'. Dr Torry elaborates the implications which his distinctions have for discussing these important terms which have to be part of the engagement with public authorities.

In my paper, 'At a loss for words' I attempt to illustrate the difficulty that arises for faith-based organizations when they attempt to express their identity and mission in their own language. Without their own words, or the right words, they are in danger of losing their distinctive presence. At the same time, the traditional way of expressing a Christian self-understanding in the language of narrative which is always particular and concrete is hard pressed to find a hearing in a public context which favours general and universal terms. Not only the dominant culture of universal rules and common standards inhibits the self-presentation of the faith-based organization. The limitations in the methods of some scientists and styles of research are such that the distinctive faith element is filtered out. Adjustment to the legalistic language of standards and criteria is necessary, but it is also important that people of faith and their organizations not lose the confidence and the capacity to tell their stories in the manner in which stories are best told. They must retain the authorship of their own narratives lest they be super-narrated by the legislation.

If finding the right words is the focus of this collection, then Michael Barnes adds a further level of complexity in his discussion of philanthropy. There are some internationally known figures who stand out by virtue of their wealth and their willingness to share it with others. But what are their motives? Beginning with the mixed motives of the philanthropist, Dr Barnes explores the extraordinary human impulse which seeks the good of the other. Drawing on two contrasting religious traditions, Islam and Buddhism, he presents a profound similarity in their ideas on philanthropy. One points to an 'exterior dynamic' of remembrance and gratitude, while the other is much more dependent on an interiority which finds its motivation arising out of a sensitivity to the interrelatedness of all things and all sentient beings. His argument is 'not that somewhere "deep down" these ideas are the same or similar or analogous – though it would indeed be strange if they turned out to be completely incommensurable. Rather, the sounds made by one conceptual world produce resonances or echoes in the other; they do speak to each other. The interest lies in understanding the source and nature of that mysterious harmony.' His exploration of these religions illustrates very well the point made in my paper about the religious reliance on a language which is concrete, full of images, and tells a story. 'Religions are nothing if not complexes of story and symbol, ritual and tradition, which form people in a particular way and enable them to make sense of their lives. Religions provide ideals and models which motivate and support certain types of behaviour'. These papers and the Words in Action project should strengthen our resources for telling our stories in our own words, and with the right words.

Patrick Riordan SJ
Associate Director
The Heythrop Institute for Religion, Ethics and Public Life

MALCOLM TORRY

VOLUNTARY, RELIGIOUS AND FAITH-BASED ORGANIZATIONS: SOME IMPORTANT DISTINCTIONS

VOLUNTARY, RELIGIOUS AND FAITH-BASED ORGANIZATIONS: SOME IMPORTANT DISTINCTIONS

Malcolm TORRY

Reverend Dr Malcolm Torry is Team Rector in the East Greenwich Team Ministry and Site Chaplain with the Greenwich Peninsula Chaplaincy. He is author of Managing God's Business: Religious and Faith-based Organizations and their Management.

If two things are not the same then 1. being clear about the distinction between them, and 2. describing the distinctions between them, can aid understanding. So, in the cause of understanding the situation which faces us in relation to religious and faith-based organizations, I intend to discuss a series of distinctions: between voluntary and religious organizations, between religious and faith-based organizations, between what I call 'attached' and 'wandering' faith-based organizations, between the secular and the religious, between the public sector and the voluntary sector, and between the public sector and the religious sector. I shall then explore the implications of these distinctions for discussion of the terms 'public benefit' (the Charities Act 2006 criterion for charitable status), 'inclusion' and 'social cohesion' (frequently expressed public sector goals for society).

Voluntary organizations

I take as my starting point that there are three sectors of organizations: private, public, and voluntary: but this doesn't make it easy to define the categories. If an organization is any structured group of people pursuing a common goal, then a private sector organization might be defined as one designed to benefit financially the private individuals who own it (whatever other purposes it might have), a public sector organization might be defined as one designed to benefit the public (and owned by the public at large through local, regional or national government structures), and a voluntary organization can be understood either positively or negatively: either as an organization established and closable by private individuals and which doesn't distribute profit to them, or as an organization which is in neither the public nor the private sector. These definitions are all contentious, and many organizations don't fit easily into a category. Is a medical General Practice in the private or the public sector? It is a partnership and profits are distributed, but all or most of its funds come from taxation and its activities are governed by government regulation. Is a primary school in the voluntary or the public sector? It has its own board of governors with considerable powers, but the state can appoint new governors if it wishes to, and all or most of the school's funding comes from taxation. Is a religious radio station which has never distributed profits to its shareholders in the private or the voluntary sector?

Even if we're not entirely happy with our set of sector definitions, we have some idea what a voluntary organization looks like, and one method of definition is to choose an organization definitely in the category (a 'prototype') and then ask if other organizations are sufficiently like it to put those into the category too. The National Trust is a voluntary organization. It is governed by trustees, it has members who pay subscriptions, and members elect trustees. It distributes no profits and it is not controlled by government (except in relation to regulated activities). Organizations sufficiently like the National Trust are in the voluntary sector.

Voluntary organizations and religious organizations[1]

I take as my starting point that religious organizations are voluntary organizations. Of course, this isn't always the case. A religious broadcasting station can be a private sector organization, and a hospital chaplaincy is in the public sector – but, in general, religious organizations are constituted by their members, they select their own governing bodies, and they don't have owners to whom profits are distributed.

But are we clear what we mean by 'religious organization'? For the purpose of this paper (and for this purpose only) I take as my working definition that a religious organization is an organization the primary purpose of which is corporate worship. If we approach the problem by employing a congregation as our prototype, then we arrive at the same result. An organization is a religious organization if it is a gathering of people engaged in worship. This definition does not in itself imply a continuing organization, because a congregation can be a once-off gathering for worship (for instance, to commemorate a particular anniversary in the context of an act of worship); and a congregation which meets at the same place and at the same time each week will not be the same congregation from one week to the next because different people will constitute it – but let us go with the definition and see where it gets us.

In a derivative sense a Methodist church, or a Pentecostal church, or a Church of England or Roman Catholic parish, could be defined as religious organizations, because their main purpose is gathering for worship (leaving to one side for the time being the ambiguity in the word 'parish', which has both territorial and organizational meanings). Immediately we find ourselves facing some interesting questions about the characteristics of these religious organizations.

First of all, the concept of membership is problematic.[2] In some churches membership is quite closely defined, but even here the concept is problematic. Is someone who holds a Methodist membership ticket but who never attends still a member? In some churches, such as the Church of England, there is no definition of membership (the use of the term on the Electoral Roll form is entirely circular; you are asked to declare whether you are a member of the Church of England, and by ticking the box you join the nearest thing the Church has to a membership list; and in this context baptism does not define membership, because that's dealt with in a separate box). The concept of membership which the Church of England now employs in practice is 'attendance at corporate worship at least once a month': a definition increasingly employed to collect statistics and to determine how much each parish should contribute to central funds. This definition coheres well with our definition of a religious organization as 'people gathering for worship', but it leaves rather vague the parish's organizational boundary. A problematic concept of membership is one of the distinguishing features of religious organizations not shared by other voluntary organizations in which membership is usually closely defined, generally by the payment of a subscription.

Another difference between religious and other voluntary organizations is the number of functions located in the clergy. In other voluntary organizations the categories of governors (usually trustees), management (paid or voluntary), workers (paid or voluntary), members (those committed and subscribing to the organization, benefiting from its services, and often electing trustees) and users (those benefiting from the organization's activity) can overlap, and, for instance, there is a growing trend to elect or appoint users to governing bodies. But it is

---

1 For a thorough discussion of the definitions of religious, faith-based and voluntary organizations, see Torry, M., *Managing God's Business: Religious and Faith-based Organizations and their Management*. Aldershot: Ashgate, 2005, ch. 1.

2 See Torry, *Managing God's Business,* ch. 8, for a thorough discussion of issues relating to membership in religious organizations.

unusual for someone to fill all of the possible roles (and, in particular, paid management or staff usually can't themselves be trustees). In a Church of England parish the Incumbent is a paid religious functionary, is not only a member of the Parochial Church Council but is its Chair, and is a member (understood as above, though interestingly without a vote in elections). In any other charity the combination of these roles would invite a Charity Commission inquiry, but no-one questions it – and independent free churches registered as charities are now asking why their pastors can't be both trustees and paid. They have a case. Such an unusual combination of roles seems to be a distinguishing feature of religious organizations.[3]

It all comes down to religion being a unique activity, and I use that word advisedly. I'm not here talking about internal religious states, because those are impossible to relate to organizational realities. By effectively defining religion as what we do I have constructed a definition of religious organizations which reveals their strangeness and which suggests that they should be regarded as a category of their own, either as a subcategory within the category of voluntary organizations or as an organizational category separate from that of voluntary organizations.

An important consequence of being able to distinguish between religious and other voluntary organizations is that we need to take care not to transfer practices from one category to another without asking whether they are appropriate. This is particularly important in relation to management methods. Not only should we not unthinkingly transfer management methods from the private or public sectors to the religious sector, but we shouldn't unthinkingly transfer management methods from the voluntary sector either.

And similarly, not only shouldn't we transfer evaluation methods, indicators or language from the private or public sectors to the religious sector, but we shouldn't unthinkingly transfer them from the voluntary sector either.

Religious and faith-based organizations[4]

I take as my working definition of a faith-based organization an organization the main purpose of which is not religion but which is related in some way to a religious organization or tradition.

Such organizations will share some of the characteristics of religious organizations and some of the characteristics of secular organizations operating in the same field as themselves. For instance, a church school is a faith-based organization because its main purpose is education but it is closely related to a religious tradition. Worship and religious education will take place and religious functionaries will be members of the governing body, so it shares some of the characteristics of a religious organization; but it will teach the national curriculum and will in many other ways be like state schools which are not church schools.

We can envisage a spectrum strung out between religious organizations (congregations) at one end and secular organizations at the other, and we can locate a faith-based organization on the spectrum. If the characteristics which it shares with religious organizations are more determinative of its activity than are those which it shares with secular organizations then it will be nearer to the religious end of the spectrum, and if the characteristics which it shares with secular organizations are more determinative then it will be nearer to the secular end.

What is important for our purposes is that we should distinguish between religious and faith-based organizations. They are not the same; and, in particular, faith-based organizations will experience tensions not experienced by religious organizations. It is these tensions which lead to our next distinction.

Faith-based organizations: the 'attached' and the 'wanderers'

Research in the United States has shown that organizations which relate to each other become like each other.[5] This is no surprise. If faith-based organizations recruit staff from secular organizations then they must expect the presuppositions and methods of secular organizations to arrive with those staff members. If faith-based organizations seek funding from secular organizations then they have to use methods, language and criteria imposed by secular funding bodies. If faith-based organizations work in partnership with secular organizations then they will need to employ methods and language coherent with those used by secular organizations – and secular organizations will need to employ methods and language coherent with those used by faith-based organizations. Because most funding and most professional training come out of a secular context we would expect more secular ideas and methods to arrive in faith-based organizations than we would expect more religious ideas and methods to arrive in secular organizations; and because government regulation and government funding streams are essentially secular, the language and evaluation methods of secular government organizations will infiltrate the most religious faith-based organization. The more secular ideas and methods arrive in a faith-based or-

---

3 For a thorough discussion of the governance of congregations, see Torry, *Managing God's Business*, ch. 6.
4 On this distinction, and on how faith-based organizations function, see Torry, *Managing God's Business*, ch. 7.
5 DiMaggio, Paul, and W. Powell, 'The Iron Cage Revisited: Conformity and Diversity in Organizational Fields', *American Sociological Review* 48 (1983) 147–160.

ganization, the more that organization will be pulled in a secular direction and the more it will become like secular organizations in the same field.

To take an example: Up to the mid-1980s the Carr-Gomm Society was a small housing association specialising in housing people coming out of mental hospitals. The Society provided rooms in large houses, and each house had a housekeeper. A small central staff worked from a dilapidated terraced house in Bermondsey. Trustees were mostly committed Christians, and a certain amount of explicitly religious activity took place. But then 'care in the community' became the vogue and the Government started to close large long-stay mental hospitals. As there were few housing associations experienced in the field, the Carr-Gomm Society found itself expanding rapidly. Its fairly new Chief Executive was an ordained minister of the Church of England, but he had been recruited from a social services post; and large numbers of new staff, new offices, and lots of government funding, pulled the organization in a secular direction. It is still an excellent housing association. It is difficult to say whether it is still a faith-based organization. It is this kind of organization which I call a 'wanderer': it has travelled a significant distance along the spectrum from religious to secular.

But not every faith-based organization is like this. The Southwark and London Diocesan Housing Association was established to enable church land to be employed for social housing, the land remaining under the control of the dioceses. The two co-chairs are Archdeacons and there are other substantial links with the two Anglican dioceses of Southwark and London. Whilst funding comes from government sources, land comes from the church; and whilst staff belong to a housing association professional world and there are close links with other housing associations, links into religious organizations (and here I count a diocese, being a federation of congregations, as a quasi-religious organization) ensure that the organization can't travel very far in the secular direction. This is an example of an 'attached' faith-based organization – though it is conceivable that future changes might enable it to 'wander'.

Similarly with the Greenwich Peninsula Chaplaincy. This was established by the faith communities of Greenwich to provide a chaplaincy service to workplaces on the Greenwich Peninsula and to manage a building on the peninsula for faith communities to use for worship, prayer, education and community development. All of its trustees are active members of the borough's faith communities and its chaplains are recruited through the borough's faith communities. Its activity is religious. It does pastoral care, not counselling. (This distinction is crucial, and requires a paper of its own.) Its funding has come from individual donations, from faith communities, and from the Community Development Foundation: strictly speaking government money, but channelled through a fund employing evaluation criteria designed specifically for faith communities. Crucially, no money has been received from the companies with which the chaplains work or from the local authority. (The temporary building and then the permanent building which the chaplaincy will manage will be provided by the developer in accordance with Section 106 obligations.) The Greenwich Peninsula Chaplaincy is thus firmly connected to the borough's religious organizations, and there are few forces pulling it in a secular direction. It is an 'attached' faith-based organization.

Of course, 'attached' and 'wanderer' are relative terms. No faith-based organization is entirely immune to secularising forces, and no previously faith-based organization entirely loses contact with its roots: but the terms are useful because they enable us to evaluate what's happening to an organization and, as we shall see below, they enable us to ask about the appropriateness or otherwise of evaluation language, methods and criteria.

Secular and religious

We have identified the two ends of the spectrum along which faith-based organizations might travel as 'religious' and 'secular'. This is a fundamental distinction clearly worthy of discussion, and up till now we haven't done that. What we mean by 'religious' and 'secular' in the context of this paper is 'religious organization' and 'secular organization'. We have been able to define a religious organization in terms of a congregation gathered for worship without defining religion. Similarly we have discussed secular organizations without defining the term 'secular'. I do not intend to discuss the terms 'religious' and 'secular' here, except to say that when we do come to discuss those terms we might seriously consider defining them in organizational terms. If it is true that internal religious states and other aspects of individual religion in the end rely on corporate religious activity, either past or present (and I believe this to be true), then it will be helpful to define 'religious' in organizational terms because we shall be less likely to fool ourselves that all is well with religion. If specifically religious practice collapses then individual religion will wither or become so indefinable as effectively to have expired. If that happens then we shall no longer need the term 'secular' because 'secular' is a derivative term: it means 'not religious', which is why it defines the other end of the spectrum. It carries no positive meaning of its own. So let secularists beware: without religion they don't exist. But also let the religious beware: it really does matter that links between the churches and other social institutions are weakening, because this constitutes secularisation. It really does matter that religious practice is declining – for this means that religion is declining. Proclaiming an individual gospel simply isn't sufficient. Rebuilding congregations is essential. And what's equally essential is creating faith-based organizations. They will wander. That's an inevitable process. We must let them go and not mourn them. They will do useful secular work, and will never entirely lose the consequences of their roots. What we must do is create new faith-based organizations, and we must do it all the time. Some might remain attached for a while, but all or most will wander sooner or later. That doesn't matter as long as there is a constant supply of new faith-based organizations coming along behind them: for as long as it remains faith-based each of those organizations will contribute to the rolling back of secularisation and to the re-Christianising of society – or, in the case of other religious traditions, to the re-religionising of society in a wide diversity of ways. Given that there is a limit to the number of religious organizations, it is in fact essential to let go of faith-based organizations. Every religious organization has its limits. One housing association to find trustees for, one chaplaincy to organise, one youth club to staff with volunteers.... If there's to be new faith-based activity, and particularly if whole new fields are to be opened up, then we must let go of the faith-based organizations which we are already managing. The essence of religion is faith, a stepping out into the unknown: and a stepping out into organizational unknowns is a service which the Church has for many centuries provided for society at large and for every local community, and by seeking new faith-based activity to establish it will continue to provide this valuable service and at the same time re-Christianise an increasingly secular world.

The public and voluntary sectors

At this point I discuss the distinction between the public and the voluntary sectors because of the issues of 'literacy' and 'co-option' which it raises.

Voluntary organizations generally start as small groups of people getting together to get something done. They might fundraise locally for their good cause; and then, if someone hears that the local authority or a charitable pot might give them some money, they might apply, and they might discover a mismatch in the language-games which they and the funder play. The group has to learn a new language in which 'benchmark' doesn't mean a graffitied park bench, and it is the group which has to learn the new language and not the funder because the funder has the money and the group wants it.

If the application is successful then the group might find itself with a paid worker to manage; but funding never comes alone. It comes with monitoring forms to fill in, accounts needing to be inspected, minutes at meetings, PAYE payments to be made; and the forms require a language to be learnt containing words like 'outcomes', 'indicators', and the like. The organization might grow some more; the local authority might invite it to tender for contracts; and it might find itself doing work which the local social services department used to do. Now there are budgets to create, employment policies to agree, recruitment processes to check, Criminal Records Bureau certificates to obtain. Every day the voluntary organization looks more like a local authority department: doing the same things, using the same language – but providing governance for free because trustees can't be paid. Co-option has occurred and the distinctiveness of the voluntary sector has been eroded. But now at least the voluntary organization and the local authority understand each other.

Three of the trustees get tired of it all, they discover a new local good cause, they wash cars to raise some money: and the process starts all over again.

The public, voluntary, religious and faith-based sectors

Religious organizations are congregations gathered for worship. They don't themselves interact directly with the public sector or the voluntary sector except over such issues as the use of buildings. The Parochial Church Council might agree to the church building being used as a polling station; it might have to apply for planning permission for changes it wishes to make; or it might share its building with a voluntary organization. It's where its activity starts to travel the faith-based spectrum that more interesting issues arise. A church might put on a community drama and might invite local schools or voluntary organizations to join in. It might seek funding for the event, and it might therefore have to learn to speak the language of secular funders. The activity is no longer worship, so what's happened is that a faith-based organization (even if only a temporary one) has emerged from the religious organization and is relating to secular public sector and voluntary organizations.

Longer term faith-based organizations might emerge from congregations and might seek funding from a local authority, or might contract to undertake local authority work. Here the same issues of co-option arise as with other voluntary organizations, and there might also be increasing ability to communicate as links between organizations consolidate; but if the faith-based organization is an 'attached' one then its language-games will be more unlike those of other voluntary organizations doing similar work and communication might not be quite so easy. The language which the group uses will be more determined by the thought-forms of the religious tradition to which the organization is attached, and the local authority might be experienced as 'illiterate'. The recent report prepared for the Church of England, *Moral, but no Compass*,[6] identifies poor

---

6   Davis, F., Paulhus. E. and Bradstock, A., *Moral, But No Compass – Government, Church and the Future of Welfare*. Chelmsford: Matthew James Publishing, 2008.

communication between the Church and civic authorities and little understanding by the Government of the Church and of the faith-based activity which it promotes. The report complains, but there's no point. Government can't co-opt the Church (at least, not at local level), so a mismatch in languages is inevitable. Take the issue of charity registration: Parishes remain excepted charities, which means that they don't have to register as charities. This means that they get left out of surveys of charitable activity. There's an obvious answer to this: Parishes should ask to be able to register, just like everyone else. Then their activity will get counted. If the Church wants to relate better to secular organizations without being co-opted by them and without travelling along the spectrum from the religious to the secular end, then it will have to take steps of its own. A useful strategy is to create new institutions to which both the Church and secular organizations can relate. The Greenwich Peninsula Chaplaincy is such an organization. The churches and other religious organizations and faith-based organizations can relate to it, the local authority can relate to it, multi-national companies can relate to it, and other voluntary organizations can relate to it – and one important result is that new relationships occur between religious organizations and secular organizations. The initial relationship might be mediated by an organization constructed partly with that purpose in mind, but the outcome can be new direct relationships: and at the same time the churches remain insulated from co-option by secular organizations. There's no point in waiting for secular organizations to do this piece of work. We've got to do it: which means that the widespread creation of mediating organizations is an essential strategy if the churches want to be understood and want their activity to be counted.

'Public benefit', 'inclusion', and 'social cohesion'

We have explored a number of distinctions between types of organizations. We shall now ask about their consequences for the meanings of the terms 'public benefit', 'inclusion' and 'social cohesion'. Here 'meanings' is plural, as it should be.

The meaning of 'public benefit' will be different for each type of organization. For a secular charity it will mean that people with particular characteristics might be cared for, educated, advised, or helped in some other way. For a religious organization 'public benefit' means the benefits people receive by being prayed for, or by attending the sacraments, or by confessing their sins. For a faith-based organization 'public benefit' might mean a type of service to the community informed by the religious tradition concerned. Thus for the Greenwich Peninsula Chaplaincy 'public benefit' means 'pastoral care': that is, conversation which employs the doctrinal, devotional and ethical resources of the faith communities involved.

Given these differences careful communication is essential: and it is up to each type of organization to do its own communicating. We can't expect the secular Charity Commission to understand 'public benefit' in terms of prayer and corporate worship, so it is up to religious organizations to explain it – and to know that communication might not be easy to achieve. It will be easier to describe some of the subsidiary public benefit which religious organizations supply: the social capital generated by tasks undertaken in the congregation, the people cared for in the congregation, and the commitment which congregations make to communities (the churches, and particularly the Church of England and the Roman Catholic Church, are organizations which stay, often when every other voluntary organizations have disappeared). Members of congregations volunteer in other contexts at a rate higher than the average, and they are not afraid to involve themselves in the most difficult kinds of volunteering (street pastors come to mind). Such subsidiary public benefit might persuade the Charity Commission to continue to count religious organizations as charitable, but that doesn't mean that religious organizations themselves should define public benefit in those terms. Even though it might not be heard, for religious organizations 'public benefit' means primarily public worship.

For faith-based organizations the issue will be deciding where to put the emphasis. There will always be public benefit, but will faith-based organizations concentrate communication on that activity which is most closely related to their more religious activity, or will they emphasise the activity which is similar to that of secular organizations in the same field? When a church school describes the public benefit which it provides will it emphasise the daily Christian worship at its heart or will it start with its position in the league tables, or with evening community use of its buildings?

'Public benefit' might have diverse meanings, but it is not essentially problematic. 'Inclusion' is. There are types of religious conviction and religious language about gender and sexuality which are totally at odds with secular convictions and language about them. Is communication possible? The answer has got to be 'yes', both because at the heart of Christian Faith and of other faiths there is a foundational conviction about human equality which unites both religious and secular language and convictions, and also because it is essential that we make the communication happen. Whilst the problematic relationship between religion and culture is one of the difficulties which such communication faces, it isn't the only one. Different faith traditions really do differ on these issues, and different groups within each faith group differ on these issues too. For the sake of our society's cohesion we are going to have to find a way both to include the different religious traditions at the heart of our public life and to pursue an equality agenda which is, after all, ultimately rooted in religious convictions.

Is 'social cohesion' as difficult? Do religious organizations have anything at all to do with social cohesion? Yes: because in the Church 'there is no longer Jew or Greek, there is no longer slave or free, there is no longer male and female: for all of you are one in Christ Jesus' (Galatians 3:28). But in another sense no, because everyone in the Church is 'in Christ', or at least exploring the possibility – and in the Church there will be few Muslims, Sikhs or Hindus. Similarly with the Mosque. There will be many nations gathered. The Woolwich Mosque is attended by people from Nigeria, Somalia, Pakistan, India, the Lebanon, and elsewhere. This is extreme social cohesion. But they're all Muslims. There might be the occasional visitor from another faith, but that's all.

So we need to look a little wider at the ways in which the different faith communities work together (and here the Greenwich Multi Faith Forum and the Greenwich Peninsula Chaplaincy are excellent examples) and at the ways in which friendships between members of different faiths create strong bonds within the community.

Social cohesion doesn't mean that there are no differences between us, and it doesn't mean that the differences between us are diminishing. The opposite is true. London is becoming a world city, and soon all of the world's differences will be present in this one place. Such radical diversity needs to be celebrated. What social cohesion means in this context is knowing that we are all radically different, that we shall never truly know each other, that the different communities will never truly know each other, but that equality of respect, rights and responsibilities is possible and that the better we work together the better we shall know each other. That's what social cohesion means. It means the cohesion of a radically diverse society. So in the context of this particular modern slogan religious organizations have something significant to teach the private, public and voluntary sectors – and we need to communicate what we're learning.

'Social cohesion' is used widely in different contexts, its meaning will constantly diversify, and religious and faith-based organizations have an important role to play in offering their own particular take on its meaning. The term 'public benefit' is the controlling concept of the Charities Act 2006 and so is rather different. It will be defined by the courts (thus absolving the Government from dealing with the tricky issue of the charitable status of fee-paying schools), and debate will mainly be about the appropriateness or otherwise of court decisions and of the meanings of 'public benefit' which they imply. In such a context religious and faith-based organizations need to do their own communicating first. It isn't up to government or any other public or voluntary body to do it for us. It is our responsibility, and if we don't do it then we've only got ourselves to blame if our position isn't understood. As for 'inclusion', we've got some work to do.

Channels of communication

What practical steps can we take? Each borough needs a Multi Faith Forum, so that representatives of different faith communities can meet each other and thus communicate amongst themselves and also in a co-ordinated fashion with other organizations in the private, voluntary and public sectors. Each borough (and not just in London) needs a well-functioning set of Ecumenical Borough Deans, so that representatives of the churches can meet each other and communicate both amongst themselves and with organizations in other sectors.

Similarly, each region needs a faith forum (and we look forward to the new London Faiths Forum achieving some useful communication with the Greater London Authority). A London Church Leaders Group already exists, but it is time it was properly constituted and resourced.

We already have national bodies to co-ordinate the churches' voice, and for the UK and Ireland we have Churches Together in Britain and Ireland. Their work needs to be refocused on the kind of political work required to create good communication between the churches and government. And we need similar multi faith bodies.

If we don't create the necessary structures then we can't blame anyone else if communication doesn't occur.

But it's not just communication channels we need. The communication needs to be resourced. The world is full of business schools; there are degree courses, websites and journals on the public sector and its management; there are centres, websites, courses and journals on the voluntary sector and its management; but on religious and faith-based organizations, as far as I know, there's practically nothing. There are scholars and institutions involved in the field. Roehampton University encouraged my own research and has discussed the possibility of a master's degree course in the field; there is a cluster of scholarly interest around congregational studies, mainly in Lancaster; Helen Cameron at Oxford Brookes University is still working in the field; and Heythrop College's interest is very helpful: but someone somewhere needs to pull it all together. If we don't then the sector's voice will not be heard and it will be our fault.

It is surely symptomatic that I, as a private individual and on the strength of writing a book, have been asked for various pieces of work on religious and faith-based organizations and their management, and in particular was asked to contribute a working paper on religious and faith-based organizations to the Carnegie UK Trust's Inquiry into the Future of Civil Society. There needs to be somewhere to which organizations and individuals can go when they want to know about the sector. If we don't provide somewhere for people and organizations to go then we can hardly blame them for not finding it.

Conclusion

An exploration of some important distinctions has led us into discussion of the terms 'public benefit', 'inclusion' and 'social cohesion' and to proposals for a plan of action. Let us get on with it.

PATRICK RIORDAN SJ

AT A LOSS FOR WORDS

AT A LOSS FOR WORDS

Patrick RIORDAN SJ

Dr Patrick Riordan SJ is Associate Director of the
Heythrop Institute for Religion, Ethics & Public Life.

The familiar expression, 'I'm at a loss for words', is ambiguous. We can imagine using it in a context in which surprise, astonishment, or shock leaves us speechless, unable to respond appropriately. This can often be a pleasant experience, when friends or colleagues present flowers or offer some tribute which is totally unexpected. Of course, it can also be the opposite, when horror or revulsion robs us of the language which might adequately express our reaction to what we have experienced. One meaning of the expression therefore makes it equivalent to 'speechless'.

The other possible meaning of this ambiguous expression is that I am lost for want of words. This could be a play on the nursery rhyme, 'For the want of a nail, the shoe was lost.'[1] But the reality referred to here is more serious than nursery rhymes. Because I am speechless, unable to speak up for myself, I lose my case. Lacking the words to make myself heard, I do not register my presence with those who should hear me, and so I am effectively non-existent. The feminist critique of the implicit sexism in our language has made us aware of how it can deny the reality of women and of their experience, and make them invisible. 'At a loss for words' can then mean un-remarked and overlooked, excluded because not mentioned, unknown because not named.

---

[1] 'For want of a nail the shoe was lost.
For want of a shoe the horse was lost.
For want of a horse the rider was lost.
For want of a rider the battle was lost.
For want of a battle the kingdom was lost.
And all for the want of a horseshoe nail.'
Quoted by Benjamin Franklin in *Little Richard Almanack,* this rhyme makes a point about foresight and timely provision, and how major consequences can follow from minor neglect.

Faith-based organizations can be lost for words. To the extent that they have a distinctively religious inspiration for their activity, and to the extent that this motivation is not named and spoken of, it can be relegated to the nebulous regions of forgetfulness and eventually disappear. At a loss for words, faith-based organizations could lose their distinctive presence in the public space. Hence the project 'Words in Action', aiming to strengthen the resources available to faith-based organizations to speak of what they do in their own languages.

In this paper I want to reflect further on how we can be lost for want of words. There is the basic sense in which members of an organization may not be able to articulate the identity and mission of that organization, even though these may be implicit in how the organization functions. But there is a further sense in that while an organization may well have members capable of speaking coherently in religious language about its mission, those who observe as social scientists may lack the capacities to grasp the reality they are examining. The want of words may occur at both levels of practice and observation. The point here is primarily about the disciplines of the social sciences, and not about government, although that might also be relevant.[2] In particular I want to draw attention to a fundamental tension between language which is primarily universal and general, and language which is particular and concrete. There may not appear to be a contradiction, for instance, between obeying the law of love – 'love God and neighbour' – and following Christ as a model for one's life. But transposed into other categories, there can indeed be radical tension between conforming to non-discriminatory equality legislation which is universalist in its formulation and showing preference for some people because they are the ones who present themselves as to be served.

I will illustrate the point with a personal anecdote. I once worked in a Catholic school which invited pupils, and still does so, to engage in service of the poor through its 'Society for the Relief of the Poor and Aged', abbreviated as SRPA. Other Catholic schools in Ireland typically have a conference (their name for a branch) of the 'Society of St Vincent de Paul', SVDP. The original motivation for the founding of the SRPA was definitely Christian and Catholic, and this is the ethos which the school hopes to foster in its pupils. But while the name of the society may adequately reflect the kind of activity the pupils engage in, it does not express the meaning and motivation for Christians who come to the aid of those in need. By contrast, the name of the SVDP, 'Society of St Vincent de Paul', evokes for those who know or who ask about the saint, the whole point of the members' activities as modelled by this saint renowned for his dedication to the poor, seeing in them the living Christ. The activities may be similar; but the name of one society is not transparent to the full meaning of that activity, while the name of the other evokes the fuller meaning by recalling the specific saint whose inspiration and example are followed. And this contrast is reflected too in the contrast between the general language of 'relief' and the naming of a particular saint. As a result, those prospective parents or other observers of the school's activity who consult the school's brochures and website can note the additional extracurricular activity offered of 'Relief of the Poor and Aged' and fail to advert to its religious ethos. But on the other hand, there is no guarantee that observers of other schools which have a conference of the SVDP will be able to interpret the religious nature of its activity. Accordingly they will apply general categories such as the relief of the poor and aged. A transparent name might at least increase the possibility of appreciating that fuller meaning.

I begin with a setting of the problem by referring to an empirical case study. Then I look at differences in typical languages and explore the possibilities of recovering an appropriate language for the public space. In particular the tension between the general and abstract language of law-making and of science is contrasted with the particular and concrete language of narrative. Developments in moral theology are shown to reflect the recovery of narrative as its source. The intention is to reinforce the confidence with which faith-based organizations can tell their stories in the public arena.

Double Dutch: examples from the Netherlands

How do faith-based organizations function? How do they speak of what they do, in their everyday normal activities? Are the exercises of planning, resource allocation and implementation any different than in comparable secular organizations? Malcom Torry's discussion above suggests that we should expect a drift away from the religious origins of faith-based organizations towards the secular styles which condition the methods and training of social workers. Torry points to the lack of research such that there is little information available about what actually goes on in the relevant faith-based voluntary organizations.[3]

There are prior questions to be addressed. Do faith-based organizations claim to have a distinctive way of gathering and interpreting information, and characteristic approaches to evaluating that information and the options which are presented? Is there in fact an espoused culture which is distinctive and which could be tested in practice? Do the operative methods of interpretation and evaluation conform to the espoused methods, and if not, are the discrep-

---

[2] I make this point to avoid misunderstanding of the project's purpose, and to differentiate it from the focus of the report *Moral, but no Compass:* Davis, F., Paulhus. E. and Bradstock, A., *Moral, But No Compass – Government, Church and the Future of Welfare*. Chelmsford: Matthew James Publishing, 2008.

[3] Torry, M., 'Voluntary, Religious and Faith-Based Organizations: Some Important Distinctions', in this volume.

ancies intelligible, e.g. in terms of Torry's analysis of drift? But furthermore, how adequate are the research methods for establishing the espoused and operative cultures and for assessing the discrepancies? Reporting an espoused culture should not be too difficult as long as the faith-based organization has a tradition of self-presentation in terms of core values, vision and mission statements, etc., and that is frequently the case. But when it comes to establishing the operative culture of interpretation and evaluation, the methods employed by the researcher can be such that they are blind to the religious elements even as they carry through and imbue the practice of care and service. As Roy Dorey put it, we are not expected to give out a leaflet explaining our motivation even as we comply with the Lord's injunction to give a cup of cold water to the thirsty.[4] How can the action espoused by the Christian as being motivated by the voice of God be assessed by the neutral observer who seeks to compare operative and espoused values? There are definite limits here, and various qualitative research methods are more and less successful in overcoming them.

One recently published study offers some help because it compares decision making in a faith-based organization with decision making in a non-religious humanitarian organization.[5] The bodies studied are two Dutch non-governmental organizations involved in providing humanitarian aid. MSF Holland *(Médécins sans Frontières)* is a medical organization providing aid directly to people in need, most often in crisis situations. In 2004 its budget was over €75 million. ACT Netherlands *(Acting with Churches Together)* is a church based organization which does not involve itself directly in aid provision, but provides financial and other support to partner organizations in the places facing humanitarian need. In 2004 its budget was €7.5 million.

In order to study and compare styles of decision making, Liesbet Heyse draws on the literature to distinguish three different styles. The first style exhibits the logic of consequences. Instrumental rationality dominates, as means are selected in the pursuit of goals according to criteria of effectiveness and efficiency. The corresponding organizational structure is labelled administrative. Information gathering and processing is valued, and relevant experts are consulted.

The second style exhibits the logic of appropriateness. People make their decisions by invoking what they are expected to do in a typical situation. Hence, the rules of the organization are significant in communicating those expectations. The rules may be implicit, as sustained by the shared memory of previous commitments. Not rationality, but obligation dominates the thinking. Socially mediated values and not primarily consequences drive the process. The corresponding organizational structure is the institution.

Heyse labels the third style of decision making 'garbage can'. This is typical of ambiguous organizations, with decentralized decision making and unstructured processes. Decisions typically fall into place when various features coincide. Problems do not precede solutions, but pre-existing solutions may find their appropriate problem at an opportune time when decisions are made.

When these three decision making styles are used to examine decision making in the target organizations it turns out to be no surprise that the logic of consequences is found to operate in the decision making of MSF Holland, as it chooses projects in which it can deliver aid directly in response to disasters. The logic of appropriateness is found more typically in ACT's decision making, which is more about evaluating and selecting partner organizations. Of course, elements of all three styles are found in each case, and Heyse draws attention to the secondary decision making patterns which operate when the default style is blocked for some reason.

The author poses the critical question in the epilogue: 'what results of this study could be relevant to practitioners in the field?' She makes some suggestions about the benefits to be derived from people becoming aware of the decision making processes in their own organizations. Despite the implications of the title, *Choosing the Lesser Evil,* which suggests an examination of moral dilemmas in the decision making of NGOs, the author is deliberately avoiding an evaluative stance and there is a methodological commitment to simply describing the operative forms of decision making. There is no attention given to moral concerns.

Nevertheless a purely descriptive study promises some insights, since the two NGOs studied provide an interesting contrast between a purely humanitarian and a church based organization. Given the interest in the additional 'value added' supposedly provided by faith-based organizations, it would be interesting to note how this appears in a purely objective study of the operations of two contrasted organizations. While it emerges that ACT is guided in its decision making by 'socially mediated values', there is very little presented in this study to indicate that those values are particularly religious. The term frequently repeated to identify the relevant values is 'solidarity', but there is no elaboration or explanation of the concept. Does this reflect a deficiency in the methods available to the researcher for examination of the relevant phenomena?

The study reports that this Church based funding organization cultivates relationships with its client organizations which deliver the services to the people in need, and that familiarity with the representatives of those client organizations, contentment with their performance to date, and trust reinforced

4 Dorey, R., 'The Voice of God in Charitable Activity: Can it be Heard Today?' *Words in Action: Speaking in our own Words.* Institute Series 10, 2008, p. 42.

5 Heyse, L., *Choosing the Lesser Evil. Understanding Decision Making in Humanitarian Aid NGOs.* Aldershot: Ashgate, 2006.

by experience are the guiding factors in choosing to fund and continue funding humanitarian projects. Solidarity does not seem to have to extend beyond this networking dimension.

I do not rule out the possibility that the socially mediated values guiding the work of ACT are in fact deeply religious, and that the organization could give a coherent theological account of the solidarity it values and pursues. But this does not come through the study. There is one small hint, conveyed in the potted history of the organization, detailing how it arose out of an amalgamation of several Protestant Church bodies in the Netherlands. But in 2000 a clear organizational separation was achieved between the provision of services which relied on state funding, and the service provision funded completely by the Church bodies and their fund raising. It would be interesting to know if this reorganization was necessitated by the divergence of ethos and socially mediated values, or if it was required by the typical transparency and reporting requirements of state funding? Here was a major decision which merits another look. Was the split due perhaps to a phenomenon experienced by many who rely on state funding, which Heyse names 'goal displacement': 'a reporting and monitoring culture adds to the accountability and transparency of the organization's actions, but also runs the danger of becoming a goal in itself. Hence, the field workers might be more focused on filling in the forms and doing the statistics than on doing the real job' (p. 205).

Some form of qualitative research is required in order to establish the operative values in any organization. The appropriate methods often include interview and recording of espoused perceptions and evaluations which are then subjected to analysis by the researcher. That analysis will involve distinctions of types, as exemplified for instance in Heyse's work on the humanitarian organizations, and evaluation of actual performance as conforming or not to those types. But here the researcher's own espoused stance conditions significantly what can be discovered in the research. Recent discussions in the sociology of religion, for instance, challenge sociologists to own up to the methodological atheism which can be part of the assumed stance of the researcher.[6] Since unacknowledged assumptions can function as a filter to block acknowledgement and comprehension of certain phenomena any decent social science will now include the moment of self-critique in which the researcher's own stance can be investigated.

Language, general and particular

There is a debate in moral philosophy between generalists and particularists, provoked by the work of Jonathan Dancy.[7] The point at issue is whether general principles play any role in moral decision making. Dancy wants to deny that they do, and that sufficient guidance can be found in appreciating all the aspects of particular situations in order to find the right thing to do in that situation. This polarization of positions in the philosophical debate is not unrelated to the contrast I wish to draw, but I should emphasize that my recovery of the centrality of particular images, models and names in the Christian moral life is not intended as advocating a rejection of moral principles.

Particularism is a reaction to the emphasis in modern ethics on justifying norms by appealing to principles. The primary task of philosophical ethics has been to ground the rules and laws which are deemed to oblige people. As Kant so stringently insisted, it is a formal requirement of a norm, if it is to qualify as a moral law, that it be universalizable, i.e., that it be capable of being applied to all who find themselves in the relevant situation. The grounding of rules of behaviour as moral laws became a key activity for ethics. And since altruism, concern for the wellbeing of others was considered a core element in a distinctively moral (and not simply prudential) stance, the justification of obligations towards other unknown people became significant.[8]

In Utilitarian ethics the greatest happiness principle functioned in this task of justification. Those actions (or rules) were deemed moral which were oriented to bringing about the greatest happiness of the greatest number. It was not a completely satisfactory argument, as evidenced by J.S. Mill's personal struggle to find a way to bridge the gap between the motivation towards one's own happiness and the (wished for) motivation towards the happiness of all others.

In Kantian deontological ethics the analysis refined ever further the nature of the formal requirement of universalizability. But the generation of material moral norms became ever more problematic. The formulation of such norms relied on terms which introduced non-formal elements which tended to link to particular situations, persons and actions. The analysis became useful as a method to filter out norms of action which could not qualify as moral, but seemed sterile as a method for generating moral norms. Hence the debate developed into an investigation whether there were indeed any exceptionless moral norms, with the resultant sophistication in nuanced formulation.

This emphasis on the justification of norms as the basic concern of philosophical ethics created the filter through which the medieval discussion of the natural law was received into modernity, namely, as a method for grounding

---

6 Sweeney, J., 'Revising Secularization Theory', in *The New Visibility of Religion*. Edited by Ward, G. and Hoelzl, M., London: Continuum, 2008, forthcoming.

7 Dancy, J., *Moral Reasons*. Oxford: Blackwell, 1993; *Ethics without Principles*. Oxford: Clarendon Press, 2004. See also Hooker, B.W., and Little, M. (eds). *Moral Particularism*. Oxford: Oxford University Press.

8 See for instance the debates gathered in *Altruism*. Edited by Paul, E.F., Miller Jr., F.D. and Paul, J. Cambridge: Cambridge University Press, 1993.

moral norms in an account of rational human nature, which being the shared reality of humankind was already universalist in form. The identification of key premises in the account of natural law in the literature (facilitated by the translations of certain succinct passages in Aquinas) led to the establishment of fundamental norms from which more material and particular norms could be derived. In one move the received idea of natural law became a rival to the Kantian categorical imperative. The fundamental premises of practical reason were taken analogously to the principle of non-contradiction in theoretical reason to be the foundation on which further material norms could be established. The metaphysical categories of substance, animal and rational, applied to humans, allowed the elaboration of various levels of the human good, in which corresponding norms could be grounded. The big challenge was similar to that brought against the Kantian approach. It was to point to the failure of the natural law to actually generate agreed norms which could be applied universally. The incorporation of culture-bound descriptions of human nature undermined further the claim to universality. The reception of natural law via the lens of Kantian universalism was a misunderstanding of medieval natural law thinking, but it reinforced the emphasis on justifying norms.

Now philosophical ethics is gradually distancing itself both from the description of the task of normative ethics and from the dominance of the deontological vs consequentialist debate. The task description of justifying norms is now seen as one task, and certainly not the only, or the most important or fundamental task of philosophical ethics. Recovery of virtue ethics as well as the exploration of the human good has relativized the concentration on rules. And if the justification of moral rules is not the only task then there is no need to be constrained by the traditional polarization between Kantianism and Utilitarianism. Freed from the preponderance of the universalizability of norms, moral philosophers have been free to explore particular obligations, not just as exceptions to universal norms, but as central to the living of a moral life.

Another possible approach is that taken by the German philosopher, Robert Spaemann who offers a new account of Aristotelian *eudaimonia* as the end of a good life. His translator Jeremiah Alberg renders the German original *das Gelingen des Lebens* as 'a life which turns out well'.[9] Spaemann is one of several recent authors whose work restores the good life, the life which has turned out well, as the main object of ethical reflection. Spaemann explains that 'the turning out well of a life is not a particular goal, in relation to which other contents of volition are degraded to mere means' (14). Instead he presents it as a horizon within which particular projects and goals can find their place and meaning.

The usefulness of considering ethics in terms of a life which turns out well avoids the concentration on law or rules to guide action, or on the outcome of action, or on the characteristics of agents which are conditions of action. It can encompass all of these without having to be confined to any one of them. It can provide an integrating context in which the traditional discussions of rules or outcomes or virtues can continue without the ideological commitment to a position which sidelines other important discussions.

The perspective of the good life, the life which turns out well, could be an enrichment for ethics. However, it is questionable whether this perspective is attainable in practice through philosophical reflection alone. Since no moral agent ever comes to regard her completed life as a whole, our primary experience for this perspective is given through our membership of some community in which we learn to consider and evaluate the completed lives of others. This learning is mediated through the relationships we have with significant others, especially parents and teachers. But biographers, artists, dramatists and novelists play their part in enabling us to consider life as a whole. Because of this shared cultural wealth, individual actors can imaginatively enter into a consideration of their own lives as wholes. Faith communities which rely on a divine narrative for the context of their consideration of human life as a whole are particularly important in this regard. They provide the resources which allow individuals and groups to tell their own stories, in fact, to write their own stories in the drama of living out their lives.

Christians who struggle to live a life of fidelity and love can draw on the traditional forms which have their sources in scripture. *The Imitation of Christ* is not simply the title of a guide to an ascetic life, a discipline for growing into Christian maturity. It is the programme for the whole of a Christian's life. To follow Christ is to imitate him. St Paul's Letters contain this injunction frequently and advise readers that they be conformed to Christ, that they exhibit the same *morphé*. And within the Church's tradition there have been found various and differing ways in which believers attempted to imitate Christ: some in lives of prayer, some in lives of service, some in combinations of contemplation and action. Augustine, Benedict, Brigid, Francis, Clare, Dominic, Ignatius, Theresa, Mary Ward, Mother Teresa of Calcutta… The list goes on and on. And of course members of other Churches and adherents of other faiths will have their own lists of names of those who modelled a life well lived. What they all exhibit is the particularity of the forms of life in which Christians and others have pursued and realised the good.

In telling our story and identifying our motivations we rely primarily on concrete narratives and only secondarily on general norms. Edith Wyschogrod relies on this contrast to highlight the importance of narratives of lives of saints

---

9 Spaemann, R., *Happiness and Benevolence*. Translated by Alberg, J., Edinburgh: T&T Clark, 2000.

(defined as exemplars of compassion). She compares didactic fables and the illustration of general laws by examples with the presentation of a narrative.

> The fable or purely didactic story is actually an argument and the moral, a conclusion arrived at deductively. But the essential structure of *narrative* is to bring something to fruition through its temporal development. The moral lesson of the didactic tale is alien to narrative as such, interrupts its flow, and remains a dead element within the story.[10]

She continues by making the same point about illustrative examples:

> In true narrative discourse the chronological character of events is integral to the story's point, whereas in the relation of theory to example the independence of the example – its own coming to temporal fruition – is suppressed in the interest of theory, an abstract formulation having general import.[11]

This is significant for the account Christians might wish to give in their own words as to what they do and why they do it. As a result, their language will be always in some sense particular. But as such it will be in tension with the universalist language which predominates in public culture, especially insofar as that culture is shaped by law and its application. There the pressure is to ensure that there is no deviation from the standard, since any such deviation is likely to follow from a discrimination in favour of some and against others.

Different, not deviant

Many philosophers of law have emphasized the importance of universality as a characteristic of law. J.J. Rousseau and F.A. Hayek might not agree on much, the former a committed republican, the latter a staunch liberal, but they both insist that generality is essential to the law. Insofar as civil law is oriented to securing a public realm and preventing those disruptions to human society which are destructive of human wellbeing it must rely on general formulations which exclude and prohibit certain actions. Murder, theft, rape, bodily harm, fraud, perjury etc. must be ruled out.

General prohibitions are important for securing the minimum of order which must be achieved if social existence is to be secured. Their negative formulation ensures that violations can be easily identified. But for indicating the myriad ways in which human individuals and their groupings can flourish, general prescriptions must remain so vague as to be unhelpful. 'Be well, do good, love your neighbour' are directives for life which can only make sense if they are exemplified in instances of wellbeing, good action and neighbourliness. And for the many possible ways in which these can be exemplified there are many narratives and stories. The nurse, the teacher, the plumber, the engineer, the policewoman, the judge, the doctor... can all appear in the relevant stories. They all have their own ways of being well, doing good and serving neighbour, and that is not merely because they have different professions. They have particular and distinctive ways of fulfilling the positive prescriptions of moral law.

Moral theologians are facing the challenge of speaking out of this experience of being different but not deviant, living the Christian life in different ways. Drawing on the image of a narrative as exemplified in a pilgrimage, a different telling of the moral life is made possible than by the sterile juxtaposition of consequentialist or deontological groundings of norms. The authors of a recently published introductory textbook for Catholic moral theology attempt the revision by drawing on the experience of living Christian life and worship.[12] The integrating image is of the Christian life as a journey, undertaken by a community of disciples, who find themselves gathered for worship. Worship, the liturgy, and related practices of the Christian life, are explored and mined for the resources needed for following the way of Christ. The editors point out how this gives their style of moral theology a very different look from the usual presentation of alternative theories for generating principles to guide decision making. This way of doing Christian ethics is situated, and the sense of being in a tradition is emphasised.

The central role of liturgy and Christian practice is sustained remarkably well through the various contributions from different authors. For instance, the experience of sharing in the Eucharist provides a very different perspective on material goods for consumption than that current in consumer culture. The sign of peace in the Eucharist and the mission to go forth bringing peace locates a discussion of Christian pacifism. The sacramental context of healing and reconciliation provides a radical and challenging view of medicine and bioethics, very much in contrast to the dominant model of scientific medicine. These discussions show how a distinctive approach to moral reflection beginning from the practice of Christian life and liturgy contrasts with an approach which shares the assumptions of secular social sciences.

Exemplifying the point about the concreteness of the Christian's story, this style of doing moral theology finds a powerful source in the autobiographical

---

10 Wyschogrod, E., *Saints and Postmodernism. Revisioning Moral Philosophy*. Chicago: University of Chicago Press, 1990, p. 8.

11 Ibid.

12 Matzko McCarthy, D. and Lysaught. T., eds. *Gathered for the Journey. An Introduction to Catholic Moral Theology*. London: SCM Press, 2007.

reflection of Cardinal Bernardin whose life and practice illustrated his consistent ethics of life.[13] Especially the challenges which the Cardinal faced in dealing with false accusations of sexual abuse of a seminarian, and in dealing with the pancreatic cancer which eventually killed him, illustrate how prayer was a real source of strength for him as he sought a different way to be reconciled with his accuser, and to be reconciled also with his cancer. This theological reflection on the lived experience of Christians gives content and reality to ideas which otherwise can seem purely idealistic and aspirational when formulated only in general and abstract terms.

Finding the right words to say who we are, and what we do, and why we do what we do, may require of us to have the courage to tell our stories. Doing so in the language appropriate to the story, in the concrete and particular images and names and memories which apply, does not preclude also meeting the requirements of legislation which inevitably are general and abstract in their formulation. What charitable organization can afford to refuse to conform to the prescriptions of the Charity Act 2006? So mastery of the relevant language is basically secured. But the failure to remember and to tell the story can leave us lost for want of words, at a loss for words. Hence the importance for religious and faith-based organizations to retain authorship of their own narrative, so as not to be super-narrated by the legislation.

13 Bernardin, J. Cardinal, *The Gift of Peace*. Chicago: Loyola University Press, 1997.

MICHAEL BARNES SJ

ECHOES OF THE OTHER – THE CULTURAL AND RELIGIOUS ROOTS OF PHILANTHROPY

ECHOES OF THE OTHER
THE CULTURAL AND RELIGIOUS ROOTS OF PHILANTHROPY

Michael BARNES SJ

Dr Michael Barnes SJ teaches interreligious relations at Heythrop College and runs a small dialogue centre in Southall, West London

Bill Clinton's book, entitled simply *Giving,* is long on stories about generosity, compassion and reconciliation but distinctly short on analysis. At the end he raises the question: 'Why do some people give so much while others give the bare minimum or not at all?' and continues 'I've thought about this a lot'.[1]

If he has, he manages to keep quiet about it. We get less than three pages which touch rather vaguely on the moral imperatives taught by religious traditions and end up with a few clichés about our 'interdependent world' and 'common humanity'. Of course, the book is not intended as a philosophical treatise on the human condition; its value lies with the examples – not just the few hyper-rich but the thousands upon thousands of selfless individuals who, for one reason or another, give money, time and skills for the sake of good causes, from HIV clinics in Cambodia to building projects in post-tsunami Sri Lanka. Clinton has written an exhortation with the message that ordinary people can do extraordinary things. The disappointment is that he does not reflect on the motivations behind the current explosion in philanthropic activity.

This is hardly surprising. There are many reasons why people want to give away their money – not all of them purely altruistic. Bill Gates talks about every life being of equal value. Warren Buffett seems more concerned to avoid the corruption of wealth. Clinton himself says he feels gratitude for what he's got and wants to give something back. There are mixed motives and skewed motives. Richard Branson enjoys playing the hero, while Princess Diana wanted to be the 'queen of hearts'. There are those who find themselves prone to guilt, those who are moved by a deep compassion for the poor, and those who just

---

1 Clinton, B., *Giving: How Each of us can Change the World.* New York: Knopf, 2007, p. 207.

enjoy the buzz it gives them. There's the power factor and the vanity factor. 'I look good when I'm standing on my wallet', was one remark quoted to me.

In this brief paper I want to reflect on the cultural and religious roots of philanthropy. I do not intend to delve into the murky realms of the human psyche. My concerns are more general. Clinton notes that some people give 'out of religious or ethical conviction'. But the link between religion and ethics is complex. What people believe clearly has an effect on what they do; religions are nothing if not complexes of story and symbol, ritual and tradition, which form people in a particular way and enable them to make sense of their lives. Religions provide ideals and models which motivate and support certain types of behaviour. It is obvious, however, that religion does not always result in good behaviour, or even properly ethical behaviour. All religions teach some version of the cardinal virtues – prudence, justice, temperance, fortitude – and provide some moral vision of humanity transformed. But the process of transformation, the movement from the reality to the ideal, is rarely straightforward. Religions have produced some of the most sublime creations of the human spirit but have also been responsible for the most appalling atrocities. Lists of precepts and scriptural texts extolling virtues and values remain at the level of slogans if they fail to penetrate the inner life of a community.

What interests me are the 'deep structures' of religiously inspired action – in both its positive and negative forms. Perhaps surprisingly I feel it's easier to appreciate such structures, the 'inner logic' of a tradition, in our flaky postmodern world precisely because religions are no longer regarded as 'master narratives' providing all the answers to life's questions. The sheer diffuseness of whatever counts for 'religion' is more and more apparent. There is an intriguing ambivalence here which bears a little attention.

The French Islamicist and cultural critic, Olivier Roy, talks about the Western experience of the 'return of the religious' in the last twenty years. He is not referring to an increase in religious practice but to the more visible place religion is assuming in the public sphere. 'Religion', Roy argues, 'is making inroads into a society decreasingly controlled by the state'.[2] Religious expression today is marked by free movement, distrust of mainstream religious institutions, anti-intellectualism and a communitarian spirit. If there is one thing which holds these shifts together, it is, he says, that membership of a religious community is 'a choice, not a cultural inheritance'. The ambivalence – paradox perhaps – is that such choices tend to take people back into the funds of religious wisdom and practice which in their institutional forms they have rejected. According to Roy, we are witnessing both a breaking down of religious frontiers *and* – more subtly – a meeting of typically Western individualism, on the one hand, and traditional religious forms, on the other. If I understand Roy correctly, the point he is making is that the secular public sphere which tends to privatise religion and the neo-religious which seeks its own public space are, to put it bluntly, on a collision course.

Now if I were to carry on with Roy's article I would be taking you into some fairly tortuous terrain – the crisis of the nation state when faced with new forms of religious expression. I begin here, however, because it seems to me that Roy is pointing to an important shift in religious culture itself. In traditional religious societies philanthropic behaviour was rooted in the legal structures of the community. In other words, it was something you did without question because you were a member of that community; it was, to use theistic language, a God-given duty. Today, in a more globalized world where people tend to choose a religious path for themselves, the motivation behind philanthropic activity is likely to be rooted less in tradition than in personal commitment. Does that mean that we are inevitably caught up in a world of eclectic religious hybrids or, worse, competing forms of religious wisdom? Maybe. But I think there is an interesting alternative.

Perhaps what the shift to personal choice means is that the underlying motivations for action, the 'deep structures' which generate the great human virtues, are more palpable, more at the forefront of cultural consciousness. If so, then the question is how to understand their interaction without simply reducing them to some rather vapid cross-religious universalism.

So much by way of justification of what follows. To illustrate my argument I want to compare a couple of ideas about the virtue of philanthropy from two great 'families' of religion – the Semitic and the Indian – more specifically as they are instantiated in Islam and Buddhism. My argument is not that somewhere 'deep down' these ideas are the same or similar or analogous – though it would indeed be strange if they turned out to be completely incommensurable. Rather, the sounds made by one conceptual world produce resonances or echoes in the other; they do speak to each other. The interest lies in understanding the source and nature of that mysterious harmony.

The Jewish philosopher, Emmanuel Levinas writes:

> Like Jews, Christians and Muslims know that if the beings of this world are the results of something, man ceases to be just a result and receives 'a dignity of cause', to use Thomas Aquinas's phrase, to the extent that he endures the actions of the cause, which is external par excellence, divine action.

2   Roy, O., 'The Crisis of the Secular State and the New Forms of Religious Expression' in O. Roy, *Secularism Confronts Islam.* New York: Columbia University Press, 2007, pp. 65–90. This English version is slightly different from the original 'La crise de l'état laïque et les nouvelles formes de religiosité', in: *Esprit,* février, 2005.

> We all in fact maintain that human autonomy rests on a supreme heteronomy and that the force which produces such marvellous effects, the force which institutes force, the civilizing force, is called God.³

Levinas is writing here of Judaism as a 'religion for adults'. But his aim is to show how something of this 'austere doctrine' can be shown to apply to 'every reasonable being'. I shall return to Levinas later; it seems to me that he can help us in understanding the deep structures of religious motivation and enable us to mend the troubling gap between belief and action.

For the moment I refer to his somewhat gnomic utterances as introducing the Semitic side of my reflection. Levinas is giving an account of theism as founded on the sheer gratuity of creation and of humanity as utterly dependent on the 'otherness' of that power. In these terms human beings are not the playthings of a malevolent fate but made capable of recognising and responding to this utter transcendence. We are characterised by *responsibility*. The point comes out more clearly when we take seriously – as Levinas demands that we do – the prophetic commitment to social justice. As so often, Levinas makes his point with a rabbinic saying. '"Why does your God, who is the God of the poor, not feed the poor?" a Roman asks Rabbi Akiba. "So that we can escape damnation", replies Rabbi Akiba'.⁴ Levinas alludes in this talk to the familiar words addressed by Moses to the people as they gather to enter into the promised land. They must not forget 'the poor, the widow, the orphan and the stranger'. Those who are landless have a call on the generosity of the landed; their origins in the land of slavery should remind them that what they have now is pure gift and not to be used to exploit and exclude those less fortunate than themselves.

This dynamic of justice performed in response to the memory of God's gift is present in Christianity and, perhaps more powerfully, in Islam. For the Muslim almsgiving, *zakat*, is one of the five pillars which summarise Islamic religious practice – along with the statement of belief, *shahada*, prayer, *salat*, fasting, *sawm* and pilgrimage, *hajj*. As a legal institution, the *zakat* is a wealth tax which by being set aside for purely altruistic purposes such as the welfare of the less privileged purifies the rest of one's property. Muslims are expected to give 2.5% of their surplus wealth each year to those in need – in addition to more informal acts of charitable giving. Underlying *zakat* is the principle of *sadaqah*, which, according to Chris Hewer, is to be translated as 'bearing one another's burdens'.⁵ As in Judaism, giving to the poor redresses the social balance which has been skewed by accumulated wealth; in this sense philanthropy is rooted not in 'charity', a free giving away of over-abundance, but in recognition that all assets are held – as life itself – as a trust from God.

In other words *zakat* – like everything else in Islam - has a primarily *theological* purpose. However much it may sound like legal prescription, it is the motivation – to align one's every act and desire with the will of Allah – which counts. 'Alms are for the poor and the needy, and those employed to administer the funds; for those whose hearts have been recently reconciled; for those in bondage and in debt; in the cause of Allah; and for the wayfarer' (Qur'an 9.60). All have a claim on the generosity of the community, as various exhortations in the Qur'an make clear. 'They will question you concerning what they should bestow voluntarily. Say: "whatever good thing you bestow is for parents and kinsmen, orphans, the needy and strangers and whatever good you do God has knowledge of it"'. (2.211)

There is a clear resonance here with Moses' words in the book of Deuteronomy. Nevertheless the moral universe inscribed in the pages of the Qur'an has its own very particular religious motivation. The central demand of Islam is submission; it is God who binds all right-minded folk together and is present in every aspect of human living. 'Whatever good you do surely God has knowledge of it. Those who expend their wealth night and day, openly or secretly, their reward awaits them with their Lord' (2.275). 'You will not attain true piety until you voluntarily give of that which you love and whatever you give, God knows of it' (3.86).

'God knows'. It might seem that God is some unseen spectator scrutinising human action. That would be to underestimate the significance of the concept of *taqwa* or God-consciousness. For Muslims the purpose of all religious practice is to form a sense of being known to God or anchored deeply in God's love. Just as the fasting month of Ramadan builds up a communal solidarity which witnesses to the unity of God, so generous giving restores a sense of justice and harmony. Islam is a tradition which celebrates the God of creation, God as the first and last enlivening force which holds the whole of creation in being and invites human beings to participate in and be responsible for the fruits of God's generous love.

Now what holds the three Abrahamic religions together is this idea of property or wealth as a gift from God. In traditions which share a vision of life as purposeful, directed towards a time of judgement, the use or abuse of creation becomes the touchstone of right human living. Hence the Jewish emphasis on remembrance which Christianity and Islam can be said to inherit. People make sense of life by recalling the purpose decreed by God and enshrined in ancient memory.

---

3   Levinas, E., *Difficult Freedom: Essays on Judaism.* Baltimore: Johns Hopkins University Press, 1990, p. 11.
4   Levinas, *Difficult Freedom,* p. 20.
5   Hewer, C.T.R., *Understanding Islam.* London: SCM, 2006, p. 106.

When we shift ground towards the religions of India we find a different approach. In the *dharmaśastras,* the Hindu law-books, for instance, wealth or profit, *artha,* is one of three 'ends of life', along with *dharma,* truth or religion, and *kama,* pleasure. How to live a harmonious life in which these values can be held together? Very roughly, two ways are taught: by living in accordance with caste-status, or *state* of life, and by living according to the customs deemed appropriate for a particular *stage* of life. The ideal pattern consists of four stages – the life of the student, then the life of the householder, followed by retirement and finally by renunciation. *Artha* is appropriate to the second stage, when you seek to raise and support a family. Later, when children are grown up and gone, is the time to consider taking *samnyasa,* giving it all away and wandering off into the homeless life.

That's the ideal. In practice, of course, nothing is ever so straightforward. I used to show my undergraduate students a video of an old man debating with himself whether to follow the tradition and become a wandering holy man. There was one wonderful sequence in which his family argued with him. The daughters clearly thought he was mad, while the wife sat there with a stoical expression on her face. It was unclear whether she was looking forward to a little peace and quiet without this insufferably pious old man or she was secretly wondering who on earth would look after her when he had gone. In the end he decided that this was not the time. That's the key – recognising the right time. The 'stages' are rooted in ancient *dharmic* rituals about the marking of time – and it is not given to everyone to grasp the auspicious moment.

Nevertheless *samnyasa* remains as a formative religious institution, and it is arguable that it is the motivation behind the ascetical Indian religions, notably Jainism and Buddhism. Both began as 'renouncer traditions', reactions against the ritualism and legal traditions of the Brahmin elite. To be a Buddhist is to take the three refuges, to find 'safety' in the Buddha, the *Dharma* or the Buddha's teaching, and the *Sangha,* the community of disciples. These are the ones who, in living out the full and strict practice of the Buddha's teaching, continue to give the tradition its moral and spiritual authority. As with *samnyasa,* the monastic life witnesses to certain ultimate values – especially the all-consuming demand to give up everything for the sake of achieving *Moksa* or *Nirvana,* release from the fetters of rebirth.

This is not, however, to reduce Buddhism to a religion of meditation and 'other-worldly' inner states. The Buddha taught the 'Middle Way', the avoidance of extremes of all kinds, and his teaching is hung around with a certain moral pragmatism. Wealth as such is not evil. It is the intention with which it is used which counts. Whatever leads to that attitude of equanimity and calm which is conducive to *Nirvana* should guide the Buddha's disciples. In Buddhism whatever one does must be done with 'mindfulness', careful attention to the present moment and all that it contains. For the monks 'right mindfulness' is the heart of their meditative practice. For the lay-folk it underpins one's every action, whether keeping the precepts or giving food to the monks on their food-round.

Perhaps the easiest way to understand something of the quality of mindfulness is to see it as a practice which nurtures the twin interdependent virtues of *Prajña* and *Karuna* – wisdom and compassion. This is what characterises the *Bodhisattva,* the 'being for enlightenment', who is committed to the welfare of all sentient beings – as the Buddhist term has it. How are the two held together? A proper attention to the way things are, mindfulness of reality as it is rightly understood, opens up in human beings a sensitivity not just to one's own suffering but to the suffering of others. Compassion, however, is more than a loose sympathetic fellow-feeling. It has about it a tough pragmatic quality which has been honed not just by attention to the needs of the other but by a careful nurturing of one's own talents and abilities. The famous 'bodhisattva vow' which is implicit in so much Buddhist religious practice stems from a peculiarly compassionate wisdom – or should that be wise compassion? Let me illustrate the point with a wonderful story from the Lotus Sutra.[6]

A young man drifts away from home and loses touch with his father. Eventually, after much wandering, he finds his way back to his father's house. He has, however, forgotten the place and does not even recognise his father who in the meantime has become very rich. The father immediately recognises his son, but he realises that his son is in such a state that to reveal himself suddenly would frighten him away. Instead he hires him as a servant and introduces him to the life of the great house. The father waits patiently on the moment when he can reveal himself. This is a brief summary of the final part.

The poor son, for his part, rejoiced in such treatment but could never shake off the feeling that he was an underling. So the father bit by bit gave him more and more important work to do until at last he made him manager of all his property. In time the poor son's feelings of inferiority lessened, and the father, in anticipation of his death, called together the principal citizens to announce that the man he had taken in was actually his son and that all his property belonged to him. It was only then that the poor man realised that this very rich man was actually his father, and his joy was unbounded as he learned that his father's vast property was his own.

6   The Lotus or Saddharmapundarika Sutra, dating back perhaps to the 1st Century BCE and extant in a number of versions, is one of the most influential of Mahayana texts with its vision of the compassionate Buddha who teaches a variety of audiences through his 'skilful means'. My summary here of the parable of the lost son is based on the translation by W.E. Soothill, from the Chinese of Kumarajiva, published as *The Lotus of the Wonderful Law.* Oxford: Clarendon Press, 1930, and reproduced in *The Teachings of the Compassionate Buddha.* Edited with commentary by E.A. Burtt, New York: New American Library, 1982, pp. 141–157.

The story is about a relationship in which identity is lost and found, in which one human being engages in the altruistic work of helping another so that both can rejoice. It makes sense within a religious culture where the practice of 'mindfulness' of one's own experience forms a certain sensitivity to that of others. From such a vision, an attentive wisdom, springs compassion. But it is difficult to miss echoes of the parable of the prodigal son from Luke's gospel. There the son who has wandered off to a 'far country' thinks of the father he has forsaken. The three Abrahamic religions can be understood as different responses to a single imperative: *remember*. Buddhism has no imperative; there is no word of God to 'remember'. But there is a practice of mindful contemplation of the present moment – in which the past is somehow gathered up. The theistic traditions respond to an external or prior Word which demands a response, and constitutes human beings as responsible. The Indian religions are much more focussed on the discernment of what Raimundo Panikkar calls the 'interior dimension' of existence, attention to that elusive 'right moment'. As he puts it, 'The Indian wonders not about God or the beyond, but about the religious dimension – a dimension at once transcendent and immanent – of cosmic existence, human existence included'.[7]

Let me try to draw these strands together. I began with the mixed motives of the philanthropist. In trying to understand something of the extraordinary human impulse which seeks the good of the other I have briefly explored two contrasting religious traditions. One points to an 'exterior dynamic' of remembrance and gratitude, while the other is much more dependent on an interiority which finds its motivation arising out of a sensitivity to the interrelatedness of all things and all sentient beings.

How do these 'deep structures' work together? For a final reflection let me return to Levinas. His great work *Totality and Infinity* has as its sub-title the somewhat forbidding 'an essay in exteriority'. What Levinas tries to show is that subjectivity emerges through a constant dialogue with an otherness both related to, yet not encompassed by, the same. In exploring this dialogue he makes a crucial distinction between need and desire. Need he speaks about as 'happy dependence' which is capable of satisfaction; need reveals a lack which can be filled – by the basic necessities of life such as food and security. It remains within my power to satisfy needs; in this sense what is other is utterly dependent on me. In need I can 'sink my teeth into the real and satisfy myself'. But 'in Desire there is no sinking one's teeth into being'.[8] 'Desire is desire for the absolutely other'.[9] It is perfectly possible to live entirely out of the modality of need. But the life properly attentive to exteriority can never be satisfied with such a ruthlessly self-centred interiority. Even the satisfying of basic needs reveals the presence of the other – in terms, perhaps, of the time it takes to be satisfied, the waiting for what sometimes is beyond one's control.

As is often the case with Levinas, it is easier to tell what he is against than what he is for. His point, obscurely put but repeated insistently, is that the processes of 'ordinary living' reveal traces of an other. The question is how the satisfying of need can avoid the obsession of interiority and open up that desire which is only properly satisfied by exteriority.

How would Levinas have responded to the new philanthropy? I don't think he would have been impressed by the generosity of the Gateses and the Buffetts any more than he was depressed by the barbarism of the Shoah which affected him so deeply. What did emerge for him from his own experience (many of his close family were murdered in the death camps) is the conviction that human morality is not effaced by the failure of morality. So for Levinas it is not a question of whether human beings can be said to be 'naturally good' or 'naturally evil'. He is less concerned with 'explaining' altruism, as if it is a given quality or virtue in human beings, than with exploring the process by which human relationships go on being generated. In other words, philanthropy, benevolence or generosity does not exist apart from the prior *provocation,* the calling forth, which one person makes to another. To be avoided is the self-centred pursuit of self, in which the other is instrumentalized in a sort of Pelagian effort to will the good. To be cultivated is that willingness to be called, to become properly a subject by being *subjected* to the other.

As I have noted, contemporary philanthropists work from a variety of motives. Some are dominated by cultural and religious values; others are touched by more immediate or personal ethical motives. Maybe it does not matter that much – and that underneath the particular commitments lies a convergence of values and virtues, however they are expressed in religious or cultural terms. Levinas reminds us, however, is that it is never a matter merely of 'choice'. Humanity is not transformed by voicing deeply held convictions. Whether we see wealth as a gift from God or something more transient or – in Levinasian terms – as a call to responsibility, the question is how we respond to those echoes which the advent of the other person sounds in our world.

---

7   Panikkar, R. *The Silence of God.* New York: Orbis Books, 1989, p. 61.
8   Levinas, E., *Totality and Infinity.* Pittsburgh, PA: Duquesne University Press, 1969, p. 117.
9   Levinas, *Totality and Infinity,* p. 34.